GW01270760

Return to Sender

an anthology of poems for Elvis Presley

chosen and edited by

Tony Charles **with** Gordon Wardman

Headlock Press, 1994

Acknowledgements

All poems appear by kind permission of the authors; many of them were written especially for this book.

- **Elvis Presley** was first published in ***The Sense of Movement*** and **Painkillers** in ***The Passages of Joy,*** both by Thom Gunn *(Faber & Faber Ltd).* These two poems appear under licence from Faber & Faber Ltd.

- **Ted Hughes is Elvis Presley** first appeared in ***A Chin?*** *(Wide Skirt Press, 1991)*

- an earlier version of **Elvis and Bing in Heaven** appeared in ***The Deep End*** *(Echo Room Press, 1987)*

- **At the Public Baths** was first published in ***Chapman Magazine*** (No 54); **Solitary Way** first appeared in ***Poetry & Audience*** (Vol 32, No 1); both these poems also appear in ***Cellos in Hell*** *(Chapman publications, 1993)*

- **The Elvis Bunjee Jumpers** first appeared in ***Ramraid Extraordinaire*** (No 3)

- **Elvis Presley** will appear in Jeremy Reed's ***Pop Stars***, shortly to be published by *Enitharmon*

- **Overwhelmed with Glory** first appeared in ***The Magazine of Speculative Poetry*** *(USA)* (Vol 3 No 4)

- **Thinking of Elvis** was first published in ***The Echo Room*;**
Elvis Is a Trash Issue was first published in ***Scratch***; the latter poem also appears in ***The Newfoundland Cantos*** *(Headlock Press, 1994)*

- **Elvis Night** first appeared in ***The Echo Room***

- **Sex with Elvis** first appeared in ***Dog***

- **Elvis: The Poem** was first published in ***Flesh, or Money*** *(Littlewood Arc Press, 1991)*

- **Jarrow Elvis** will appear in ***The Bettle House*** *(Clocktower, 1994)*

Published by Headlock Press
The Old Zion Chapel, The Triangle, Somerton, Somerset

ISBN: 1 898987 03 3

Elvis Presley was The King

and that brooked no argument. Poor white boy who fused black and white trash music into a sound like nobody had ever heard before, he transformed the consciousness of a generation. He was the role model for every rebellious young male - whose rebellion was nevertheless played out within safe boundaries in the context of western society as a whole - and the sexual icon for every female. He became, quite simply, one of the most famous people in the history of the world.

His voice was brooding, bruising and beautiful; his rock n' roll drove forward with effortless power, yet he could also handle tender ballads with lyrical gentleness. His performing magnetism transcended even the most banal of film scripts and, when he returned in the later stages of his career to do the stage shows in Las Vegas, he proved against all hope that the charismatic genius was undimmed, but tempered by experience.

His life became a legend in itself; and the manner of his death - victim of his own fame - and subsequent immediate apotheosis ensured that his fame continued, grew even, thereafter. This is so not only because of the immense numbers of records he continues to sell, scorning all imitators, but also because of the refusal of thousands of his admirers to believe that he really can be dead. Hence the cults, the impersonators, the strange stories in newspapers. While I was putting this book together, a man from a small Somerset town committed suicide by taking a barbiturate cocktail. This would not in itself have been particularly remarkable except that the man in question had changed his name to Elvis Aaron Presley and had even persuaded his ex-wife to change hers to Priscilla.

The poems in this book reflect all these different aspects of the Elvis culture: biographical, homage, autobiographical, reflective and ironic, they offer an alternative collage of one of the most remarkable performers of his - or any other - age.

Tony Charles

Contents

Elvis Presley by Thom Gunn 5
Never Such Innocence Again by Rodney Wood 6
Analysing the Radio Echo/Number Crunching by Andrew Darlington 7
Charnel House Rock by John Cornelius 9
Overwhelmed with Glory by Steve Sneyd 10
Good Rockin' Tonite by Jim Lindop 11
Elvis Presley by Jeremy Reed 12
Thinking of Elvis by Gordon Wardman 13
Of Elvis Presley by John Gibbens 14
Fun in Acapulco by Ann Gray 15
End of the Track by Geoff Stevens 16
An American Tragedy by Mal Smith 17
Aaron's Rod by Ian McDonough 18
Somewhere It All Went Wrong by Tilla Brading 19
Pugno Probito by Tony Charles 20
At the Public Baths by Jim C.Wilson 21
Ted Hughes Is Elvis Presley by Ian McMillan 22
Elvis Meets Hitler by Phil Bowen 25
Idol by Genista Lewes 27
Belated Homage from a Far Kingdom by Anthony Watts 28
I Was Elvis's Secret Woman by Gwen Jones 29
Elvis: A Life in Pictures by Derek Woodcock 30
Jarrow Elvis by David Crystal 32
Sex with Elvis by Martin Mooney 33
The King Would Grin by Steve Chubb 34
Elvis and Bing in Heaven by Geoff Hattersley 35
The Most Powerful Boy in the World by Damian Furniss 36
Solitary Way by Jim C.Wilson 38
The Elvis Bunjee Jumpers by Tony Charles 39
Elvis Is a Trash Issue by Gordon Wardman 40
Elvis Night by Timothy Cumming 42

Easter Rising, 1990 by Ray Stebbing 43
Baby by Penelope Shuttle 45
Stealing the Blues by Stuart A.Paterson 46
Prestwick Airport by William Neill 48
Elvis: the Poem by Wes Magee 49
Big Sister's Former Boyfriends by Roger Elkin 50
Hound Dog by Patricia Pogson 52
Naked Gun by Kerry Sowerby 53
Missing Elvis by Frances Wilson 54
Hyperglycaemic Haiku by Hilary Mellon 55
The King of Rock and Mime by Kenny Knight 56
The Backing Band Tune Up by Steve Davies 58
Elvis Presley Discusses the Nature of Reality/Love in the Age of Intelligent Machines by Andrew Darlington 60
Painkillers by Thom Gunn 62

Biographical notes on contributors 64

Cover illustration: **Thankyou Very Much** by Dick Boulton
Endpiece illustration: **The King's Crown** by Joe Shortt

Elvis Presley

Two minutes long it pitches through some bar:
Unreeling from a corner box, the sigh
Of this one, in his gangling finery
And crawling sideburns, wielding a guitar.

The limitations where he found success
Are ground on which he, panting, stretches out
In turn, promiscuously, by every note,
Our idiosyncrasy and likeness.

We keep ourselves in touch with a mere dime:
Distorting hackneyed words in hackneyed songs
He turns revolt into a style, prolongs
The impulse to a habit of the time.

Whether he poses or is real, no cat
Bothers to say: the pose held is a stance,
Which, generation of the very chance
It wars on, may be posture for combat.

Thom Gunn

Never Such Innocence Again

I ran all the way there
to see his films, if they were 'U's,
at the Cannon opposite Marks and Sparks
and afterwards, ran all the way back.

Good, simple, innocent stuff
where the girl was always pretty
and Elvis clean as a crew cut,
I always wanted him for a brother.

When my parents were out
Old Tyme Dancing
I stayed up late with an older cousin
and his girlfriend

who kept flashing her white knickers.
He put on a stack of early Elvis
and cut the lights
before sitting next to her.

I shut my eyes and the music
took me far out to sea
where I could feel the swell
and hear the creaking sofa

urgent as a slapping bass.

Rodney Wood

Analysing the Radio Echo / Number Crunching

1958 ...

he's Elvis Presley
she's Brigitte Bardot,
with Yorkshire 50's monochrome
and role-models scarce
he lives ***Jailhouse Rock,***
a sneer to denote secret hurt
that women yearn to soothe,
an angry tenderness posed in
careful profiles of rejection
that no-one else sees
through the acne
and NHS spectacles

with Yorkshire 50s' monochrome
and role-models scarce she
defines adolescent sexuality
from French movies where
girls can pout suggestions
through beatnik hair,
bare-foot in a rage for life
that Leeds denies and
parents won't allow

1968 ...

he's married, two kids, loses his job,
she has to get married
has three kids and divorces

1978 ...

he works factory night shifts, gets drunk
watches TV bored and dead inside,
she remarries but he goes bankrupt
and works away,
he stays late in bars, drives hard,
no longer cares

1988 ...

and they finally meet at
someone's Saturday night party
where she senses a secret hurt
she yearns to soothe, and
he sees a rage for life
that Leeds has denied

and,
making love,
there's no longer
need for poses.

Andrew Darlington

Charnel House Rock

Being an imaginary message from John Lennon to Elvis Presley

Can you spare a minute
Of your precious time
I'm thinking of calling
To leave one of mine
I'm not playing no game
Forget the wealth and the fame
Don't let it put you to shame
Because we all end up the same
With only one thing to say
And I can only love
You

When you go away
Break the back of day
Staying home at night
On your own again
And me trying to bring you down
Let me apologise
Because we all end up the same
With only one thing to say
And I can only love
You

Sentimental clouds
Float across my sky
Why
I wonder why
Looking back at me
And the way I used to be
Fiery gems of anger
In my tarnished golden life
Keep me thinking
Make me move
And then I feel it
That's when I feel it
Somebody's walking on my grave
And we all end up the same

John Cornelius

Overwhelmed with Glory

still we sight him risen
Elvis with such fertile faith-ground
second coming of
Christ in this aspect has almost
beaten insectlike
Nixii to the punch their
millions coming hip-
shaking Kings into our space
urgent with passion

Steve Sneyd

Good Rockin' Tonite

When he hears of Elvis' death
                                        Lennon rants:
"He died the day he joined
                                        the army!"
by which he means the hard zip
                                        attitude,
the sideburns and the sneer lip
                                        all conjoined
(plus the mythical salami
                                        in his pants)
gave us the rebel...hero...dude.

                                        Shibboleths
were sickled flat: we'd listened to their shite.

We'd heard the news: there's good rockin' tonite.

Jim Lindop

Elvis Presley

He's photographed against a Cadillac,
one of the many littering his park,
white shoes conspicuous against the black

jacket the cliff edges around the quiff
broken by gelled strands, loose diagonals.
His posture's always informally stiff,

it seems to say, *"I am the first and last*
to make music into a religion.
My virtue is in owning to no past

and yet the present leaves me obsolete."
The antebellum facade at Graceland
has two stone lions guarding the retreat;

the rooms are kitsch, an ersatz movie set,
no sound, no light, and yet the *mis-en-scène*
describes the man: wall to wall mirrors vet

the ostentation without commentary.
A red room, blue room, chandeliers, peacocks,
each piece has no familiarity,

but suggests someone filling in a space
eclectically, obsessed by the unreal,
catching sight of himself in a surface

in which a sculpture preens. His fall was long,
cushioned by chemical supernovas.
We listen. Who is that inside the song?

Jeremy Reed

Thinking of Elvis

- this one's for The King
  You're Right, I'm Left, She's Gone
- story of my sweet life

- aye, you and me both, pal

Are You Lonesome Tonight? - the version
where he forgets the chuffing words -
didn't that say it all?
the class line on success -
when the boat comes in, the boot will follow -
gulls turned vultures feeding off
their own unfinished business,
caught, like crabs, in the mesh of the nets
That'll learn you, smartarse

I'm at a dangerous age myself,
thinks Hank,
a delayed 20th century congress
giving me fucking gip

- a midlife crisis of capitalism,
  that's what I've got, Tam; did you know
  at my age Elvis was dead?

- aye, but he's *still* dead;
  not a man in this bar couldn't give you
  an Elvis number *just like that,*
  that's seriously permanent fame

a cult for the *non-kulturny*
Always On My Mind
in the ruins of the struggle
Always On My Mind
in the fuckup of my days
Always Always On My Mind

Gordon Wardman

from **The Book of Praises.** ***In praise....***

Of Elvis Presley

Adored and
mocked respectively
for what he wasn't and was,

whether the sapling's surge and rustle
of green, inspired and flexible youth

or later dark brown
cello roundness; royal, light
or midnight blue;
whether inflated,

fattened, vibrated, in self-parodic pop,
touchingly; or driven at rock John-Henry-

like, directly; hollowness -
not emptiness but habitation
by a ghost persisted: Who said to the folk
who mocked and adored him, *"I hope I haven't bored you."*

John Gibbens

Fun in Acapulco

I had no fun at all in Acapulco
and I sat through all the songs
(my sister wouldn't go alone).

When the lights went up I told her,
"I think Elvis Presley's rubbish
and it wasn't him that did that dive."

What happened next happened quickly.
I was in two rows at once,
feeling queasy. I think she hit me.
So unreasonable. She knew
I'd always liked Cliff Richard best.

Ann Gray

End of the Track

Working on the track
forty-five cycles an hour
passing our positions;
bottom-brackets hand-sprayed,
whole frame undercoated,
top coat electrically sprayed,
followed by the varnish.
We were watching the clock
as the time neared tea-break
when the Tannoy system
installed for War Time morale
spluttered and crackled into life:
"This morning, the American singer
Elvis Presley passed away."
We stopped work and waited,
smoked our cigarettes
beneath the *No Smoking* sign,
and when the news was confirmed,
we all sang ***Heartbreak Hotel***.

Geoff Stevens

An American tragedy

1 -The Burger King

Put it this way:
  If you ran a McDonald's,
    Would you employ Elvis?

2 - Marching on

From blue-eyed boy
  To burger and barb binge.
    Glory, Glory, Halleluia....

Ladies and gentlemen,
  Elvis *has* left the building.

Mal Smith

Aaron's Rod

That ole dry stick, life
blossomed
grew strings and tuning pegs
A boy uses what's around
black mamma songs
a little shake and drawl
hey that's alright with me.

Lord, glory blows its whistle
then it steams on down the track
that miracle well
seemed so doggone deep
run dry
no no-one really here but me
runnin' to fat.

Heard tell of a tree
grows tall and fast and mean
eats the ground, man
then it turns and eats itself.
Fruit comes
big and rotten.
Hell, I'm lonesome tonight.

Ian McDonough

Somewhere It All Went Wrong

Graceland became overweight,
too heavy to carry

and the leader of a revolution
he couldn't understand

didn't fight, though in one wave
he caressed a live audience

who unwrapped him
from anonymity to circulate again

round the lounges of Las Vegas
but then, locked into his own

he was surrounded by mirrors
puppeted back into a parody of king

and it doesn't take long,
pill-popping a reconstructed
idol to perpetuity.

Tilla Brading

Pugno Probito

We had the pout, white T-shirts,
jeans and the heavy lick of hair.
No-one could sing like Elvis, though:
those covers they sold in Woolworth's,
remember? Embassy label.
After a while, we didn't try.

It was enough that he did what he did,
thrilling the summer airwaves.
His moody alchemy turned banalities
into pure gold. Geoff swore he knew a girl
who'd let him if he put ***Old Shep*** on the Dansette:
she pretended Elvis was fucking her.

There were hot days when Birmingham
could have been Alabama. Bus to the Lickey hills,
combing our hair and playing the machines, hanging cool;
swimming at the Lido, stretching out on towels
saying, *Have you seen **GI Blues** yet?*
Yeah. We sang the title song all the way to Dover.

- He could have been **the** *great white Blues singer,*
said Dave. Well, what did he know about Blues, anyway?
After we got to Florence, I met this American girl,
Carin. Her mother lived near the Ponte Vecchio
and played poker.
On an afternoon that felt like thunder,
we went to see ***Kid Galahad***
(Pugno Probito) - dubbed dialogue, but the songs were true.

At Fiesole next morning, among the theatre ruins,
I fell in love. Lizards scuttered between white rocks
And her mouth was warm and dusty, like pollen.
She pushed back my quiff and combed it for me.
She loosened my belt and slid her hands inside.
Under my breath, I was still humming the song.

Tony Charles

At the Public Baths

I paid 1/9 for a crucifix
and wore it to the Baths. The teddy-boys
echoed Presley's perfect songs, getting kicks,
as they stroked their high quiffs dry. Shower noise,
pipe rattle, steam gasps and me, at ten, white
as rice-pudding, proud in my trunks of satiny
purple and gold, thrusting my way through bright
light warm green waves, my eager limbs skinny
like milk-straws. The silvery chain clung to my
throat as I mouthed an Elvis pout; a boy,
I stood in the Shallow End. I eyed the High-
diving board, felt the purest soaring joy
of taking off. *"Next week, perhaps,"* I thought.
My cold cross dripped; my trunks felt cold and taut.

Jim C. Wilson

Ted Hughes Is Elvis Presley

I didn't die
that hot August night.
I faked it,

stuffed a barrage balloon
into a jump suit.
Left it slumped
on the bathroom floor.

Hitched a ride on a rig
rolling to New York. Climbed
into the rig, the driver said
"Hey you're..."
"Yeah, The Big Bopper. I faked it,
never died in that 'plane crash.
Keep it under your lid."
I tapped his hat with my porky fingers.
He nodded. we shared a big secret.

Laid low a while in New York.
Saw my funeral on TV in a midtown bar.
A woman wept on the next stool but one.

"He was everything to me. Everything.
I have a hank of his hair in my bathroom
and one of his shoelaces
taped to my shoulderblade."

"He was a slob," I said.
She looked at me like I was poison.
"He was too, too big," I said.
"He wanted to be small, like
a little fish you might find in a little pond."

I needed a new identity.
People were looking at me.
A guy on the subway asked me
if I was Richie Valens.

So I jumped a tramp steamer
heading for England.
Worked my passage as a cook.
In storms the eggs
slid off the skillet.

Made my way to London.
Saw a guy, big guy, guy with a briefcase.
Followed him down the alley,
put my blade into his gut
and as the blood shot
I became him,
like Momma used to say
the loaf became Jesus.

I am Elvis Presley.
I am Ted Hughes.

At my poetry readings I sneer and rock my hips.
I stride the moors
in a white satin jump suit,
bloated as the full moon.

Bless my soul,
what's wrong with me?

At night, I sit in my room
and I write, and the great bulbous me
slaps a huge shadow on the wall.

I am writing a poem
about the death of the Queen Mother
but it won't come right.

I look up. Outside a fox peers at me.
I sing softly to it,
strumming my guitar.

Soon, all the foxes
and the jaguars and the pigs
and the crows are gathering
outside my window, peering in.

I sing ***Wooden Heart, Blue Hawaii.***
There is the small applause
of paws and feathers.

I am Ted Hughes. I am Elvis Presley.
I am down at the end of Lonely Street
and a jump suits rots in a Southern coffin
as people pay their respects to a barrage balloon.

I sit here,
I can feel the evening shrinking me
smaller and smaller.
I have almost gone. Ted,
three inches long, perfect.
Elvis, Ted.

Ian McMillan

Elvis Meets Hitler

Glitz from the American's suede
was hanging above
the shorter man's moustache.
It was almost touching.

"You made for yourself
quite a noise young man.
I died before I had time."

The Führer's complexion
was as pale as Poland,
his profile Japan.
"Come across Sylvia Plath?"
"No, Sir."
"Paradise Lost?"
"Did they, Sir?"
"Yes,
To a team with only one man."

And his sigh blew down
an oak in the Balkans;
it landed an inch
in front of some Private's boot
and his thumbs drummed
a-well a-well a-wella
while the Pelvis' leather
shook a salute.

Relaxed, easy now,
they demonstrated famous steps,
gave their reasons
for leaving England alone.
Elvis mentioned nice things
said about him as a soldier.
Hitler had a go on Elvis' comb.
Always hated Daddy, he said,
but dug Mussolini during his Picasso period,
taught him to see dust
as he charcoaled his bulls.

When I interrupted them,
they were talking about getting a house together,
it would be mellow,
They'd have a drum-kit in the front room,
wanted posters on the walls.

Phil Bowen

Idol

Heartbreak Hotel was the start of it.
That's when me and my friend learned how to scream;
your swivelling hips gyrated just for us.

A pair of blue suede shoes
was enshrined on a shelf in our bed-sit
as we crooned along with you:
two wild cats, all ready to go
our money on you, our passion on show.

If your all-American heart skipped a beat for us,
we never knew, but cheek-to-cheek with the telly,
we smoothed your black cow's lick,
savoured those sardonic lips,
and almost, almost touched the sweatier parts of you.

Genista Lewes

Belated Homage from a Far Kingdom

I spent the 'fifties in the twilight zone
Where fledgling poets burn to earn their wings -
And consequently never felt the lure
Of the king with curling lip and the phallic guitar,
Who oiled the rusty joints of Western man.

The pelvic revolution dawned for me
When three gorillas of the Lower Sixth
Came rocking and rolling towards me down the corridor.
Gyrating, finger-snapping, filling the space
With loud barbaric noise, they nearly trampled me
Under their blue suede shoes. I was terrified.

With any sense, I'd have joined them. These were the ones
Who were pulling the birds while I was drafting sonnets
never to be sent to the blonde Grammar School girl
at the front of the bus, whose neck was silk and honey.

Elvis -
It's said you're still alive, which of course is true
As long as your records sell.
Accept my weary and belated homage. You
Were never my king - I limped to a different drum,
But should perhaps have rendered unto you
The part of my youth that went missing
- and never turned up.

Anthony Watts

I was Elvis's Secret Woman

Elvis was a Welshman,
though it's not widely known.
No-one can tell you like I can
how 'twas when the King took his throne.

I remember the first time in chapel
that I noticed his deepening voice -
my body ignited like kindling
and I knew, right then, he was my choice.

Rocking pubs from Tuddewi to Wdig -
weekends Aberteifi, too -
it's hard for a man to take such adulation
but I stood by him. I loved him. He knew.

I won't bore you with all of the stories
we made up, through the years, for the press.
You think he's buried at Graceland,
but 'twas at Solva I laid him to rest.

Now the rocking's all over for Siôn Fawr,
though his voice still turns me to jelly.
But I'll tell you one more thing that you didn't know:
he took his stage name from St Elvis, Preseli.

Gwen Jones

Elvis: A Life in Pictures

Marriage

A knife slides into the wedding-cake,
a sharp smile skewers his bride,
doll-like, drilled, eyes front.

Divorce

Cheeks puffed, he clings to an arm,
hidden by tinted glass, lip half raised
as if about to speak.

Graffiti in Graceland

Words on stone, scrawled
offerings always dated,
pointed walls of love.

The King with Officers

A team of sheriffs, the big star,
black-suited line-shooters
haloed by a Christmas wreath.

Statue: Las Vegas

Godlike, hands pushed sideways
for balance, guitar swinging free,
movement cast in streams.

Road sign

His sketchy face, *"NO TURNS"*
in Graceland, guitar frets
point down a one-way street.

Memphis Souvenir Shop

Elvis is a word
above *"Souvenirs"*, a candy-striped awning,
one car, empty spaces, broken puddles.

Derek Woodcock

Jarrow Elvis

short cuts across the football pitch
a lame dog sniffs around a half-burnt tyre
and the family Giro head for the tip
the youngest armed with an air gun.

Graceland is hungry. Stero smashed
the last suit in pawnshop window.

Business as usual in the corner shop
but he can't ask for credit, that's just the way it is.

Jarrow Elvis waiting for a bus
then walking home in the rain.

David Crystal

Sex with Elvis

He came upstairs in his rhinestone catsuit
for the first time, after all these years.
He even brought the towel he wore around his neck
for the show's last, sweat-breaking numbers
when he'd practise his karate on thin air.
I used to tie myself to the bars of the bed
while he told me the story of how he faked his death
to come back as my husband, an Irish lookalike
for the Vegas years; how he could choose
any number of women, but wanted me,
and how even today the fan mail was piling up
at a letterdrop somewhere in North Down -
love notes and death threats, proposals
of marriage, offers he had to refuse.

Martin Mooney

The King Would Grin

The King
Would grin
And swing
His hips

He'd smile
Awhile
And pout
His lips

The girls
Would scream
He was
Their dream

The King
Should give
Us men
Some tips.

Steve Chubb

Elvis and Bing in Heaven

Elvis likes to take things easy.
he sits by the guitar-shaped
swimming-pool in the sun,
smothering hot dogs with ketchup,
stretching his toes,
pigging King Cheeseburgers.

Bing can't stop moping.
Since that day on the golf course,
his ears have been sticking out again.
He shuffles from cloud to cloud,
asking everyone he meets
for sellotape or glue.

God has a clapperboard
he likes to play around with.
Out of respect for the old man's
cheque, Elvis agrees
to be in one of his movies.
He takes the part of a beachball

but grows churlish when God
is forced to re-shoot
due to Bing wandering onto the set
looking for sellotape or glue;
he assumes creative control
with God just holding the camera.

The angels are there
to be signed for a pittance,
used in the opening scene:
they flap their wings, Bing hides
his ears, and Elvis
gets to make love with his pants off.

Geoff Hattersley

The Most Powerful Boy in the World

Shoes cardboard lined to cover the holes,
chewing gum, guitar and overalls,
blond locks slicking towards jet black,
with a voice that roiled like the Mississippi soil;
second best at the County Fair.

Back home, Gladys Love looks on her son
and sees double - he catches the reflection
in her dark-rimmed eyes. *No bigger than a minute.*
That's Jesse staring back, floating in vitreous fluid.
Shazam! The little boy inside the growing man.

*** *** ***

Southern tan, grin slouched on his face
like a sharecropper with two bladders full
of Memphis moonshine. Hair swirled
with brilliantine, cut by the devil's own barber.
Girls swoon, boys sneer - he borrowed the shirt
and stole all the moves. No matter.
First prize at Hume High Variety Show.
None better.

They really liked me, Mom. I won!
Pride splashes like cologne on her face:
bluey-black hair and a broadacre smile,
with powder puffed on to smooth the lines.
Beer in her kiss and still in those eyes
the first-born; twice the love, double the worry.

*** *** ***

The motor of his left leg jive-jumping
like a mongoose in a sack. Lawnmower cut -
flat top, feathered tail; charcoal 'burns and
shotgun glare; pink slacks, pink shirt;
bleached buck shoes and a quiver on his lip;
a bellyful of rhythm and a headful of blues.

Pale face, black soul - the rockabilly sound;
scratchy country music with a honky-tonk beat.
Blackie rocks bass, Scotty really rolls,
high-kicking licks go straight to the feet:
Hillbilly Cat and the Blue Moon Boys,
four-dollar record worth a million bucks.

A thin white plate of raw acetate,
ten inches wide like a slab of icing
off the wedding cake his ma never had.
Happy anniversary, Mom.
Spun on the family phonograph,
his voice pipes straight to her heart,
fills the space his brother had left.

*** *** ***

And on the airwaves, the Tupelo Tornado
shears chickens of feathers and dehorns cows.
DJ's just let the needle skip repeats -
switchboards light up like Christmas trees
and fame falls into his shaking lap.

Hero of every comic book he ever read -
the most powerful boy in the world:
Captain Marvel Jr. - boy and superman.
Shazam! Old images are melted down.
Shazam! A new idol is raised.

Damian Furniss

Solitary Way

Some said the Army was his death.
But, head shorn, uniformed
and every mother's perfect son,
he rose again, warming wooden hearts.

Blue suede shoes were left behind;
through his celluloid years
and years he danced on sand,
nibbled pills and crooned.

In a cold half-empty picture-house
I kept vigil as he sleepwalked
(with wholesome girls in big bikinis)
through crass resorts and America.

And now, lost in middle age,
as gates shudder and close,
I understand his falling,
would have him rising yet again.

I'd have him return
if even just to sing soft rhymes
to trained children and grinning dogs
in Eden or Hawaii.

Jim C. Wilson

The Elvis Bunjee Jumpers

Out of the sky they come, falling like gods;
almost they dash themselves to pieces
on the small clear square of ground
before our very eyes. And then
they hurtle upward,

Twanged by the great guitar strings
that tie them to the clouds they come from;
they thunder down again, and up,
booming like fat yo-yos,
coming at last to pause in the spinning air.

They hit bright buckles to unsnap
the jewelled safety harnesses,
drop deftly like paratroopers
and move amongst us, touching
our heads and hands in benediction.

They dazzle the eye: white satin,
rhinestones, the elaborate coiffure;
some are made up, some corsetted
like the King himself when he played Vegas.
They wear sharp rings, which we may kiss.

Perhaps they sign autographs:
how do they sign?
For Tony. Elvis "The King"
(aka Billy Duddlestone) 1993
Thankyou. Thankyou very much, really.

My wish came true, like this.

Tony Charles

Elvis Is a Trash Issue

These transatlantic visits.....make me feel as if talking with Posterity from the other side of the Styx - in a century or so the new English and Spanish Atlantides will be masters of the Old Countries in all probability.

Byron

history and wilderness chasing each other
round and round the witchy woods,
a New World Avalon dreaming,
overweight and playing the slots

- hell, I've left it too late to be Lord Byron,
Tam, I'm gonna get me a hat and a steel guitar,
I'm gonna be a hat act

- yeah, well, keep your day job but,
they'll always need a good abortionist

muffdiving a comrade over my desk
back in the Alhambra House Kremlin,
leaflets sliding to the floor
- Poland, Afghanistan, Alternative Economic Strategy

- shit, I miss all that political stuff

this canto is dedicated to Elvis,
if not the hanged god, the stuffed one,
whose kingdom is all our backwaters

- he was trash like us, yeah?

- aye, trash right enough, and beautiful

somewhere between Frank Sinatra and the
Incredible String Band
a penny drops
a selection is made

Newfoundland is still a dream

Elvis is a trash issue

Gordon Wardman

Elvis Night

In dead men's cast-offs
that feel dirty and smell
of charity shops
I search and stake out
bars like these where
no one likes to talk too much
and fights start over
the smallest thing. Father in law
stands to sing ***Moody Blue.***
Mother slips into the dark
and breaking through the video screen,
Elvis in a Cadillac
with two tickets to Graceland,
the patron saint of lost souls.
I dance in my Egyptian slippers
and pass out.

Timothy Cumming

Easter Rising, 1990

At Joe Danno's Bucket O'Suds, 3123, North Cicero, Chicago.

He does not seem mad,
this young man I'm talking to,
not while he keeps hat on head,
concealing the shaven pate
with its one remaining curl,
a forelock, which he could tug
should the King, having risen again,
not three days but thirteen years dead,
walk in through the locked door.

We talk together as we watch,
in a dim light, Joe mixing cocktails
with arcane ritual to secret formulae
calling for unimaginable ingredients.
His friendly drawl and sober speech
have cadences of homespun wisdom
beyond his years. I am not prepared
for this mature sobriety in one who was,
I'm told, united to his ferret
in a marriage ceremony solemnized
at the Church of Elvis Presley, Risen King.
I forget to ask whether the bride
entered to ***Love Me Tender*** .
And did the happy pair depart
to the strains of ***So Glad You're Mine*** ?
With what happy rituals did
Hymen attend the marriage bed?

I reflect upon the mysteries of life:
Joe's recipes; why the owner of a bar
should, on a Friday night, lock the door,
switch off the sign; and how come
a youth with shaven head and ferret wife
should be talking sound commonsense
to an imprudent greybeard
more than twice his age.

Such cosmic questions will remain
alas, unanswered: The King always did
move in mysterious ways
his wonders to perform.

Ray Stebbing

Baby

Baby, glide over rivers,
kiss trees, be happy,
The readers of *The Sun*
have forgiven you everything.

They gather outside your house
in silent adoration,
getting closer and closer.
Baby? they ask. *Baby, how much rain you want?*

These tables and chairs? You want?

Baby, there are better things than these.
And when there are no more things,
no rooms, and not even the paintings are there
in the no rooms,

that's where you'll live, Baby,
nowhere, forgiving everyone everything
till you make the statues weep
as they never did when they were alive.

Oh Baby, kissing trees, being happy,
glittering like Elvis in the street,
stopping the wedding massacres with one word,
this is what you'll do,

busy with more important things than food,
sex or sleep...
Know what, baby?
It's only us impersonators that keep Elvis alive.
It's only you, Baby, no-one dares make into a movie.

Your hands hot enough to fry eggs on,
your namesake eyes like those I tried so often
to paint from memory, but couldn't.

Penelope Shuttle

Stealing the Blues

I won't forget to put roses on your grave

Jagger/Richard

I was pink-fat, blues-bitten, cow's-licked and eleven
when Elvis croaked and entered Housewife's Heaven,

bequiffed, with ball-hugging drainpipe swagger
and 50lb lighter. For Nan McTaggart,

36, Ritchie Court, Kilmarnock, our next-door
Ronette in rollers and a pinafore,

it was the wet dream dried up, the Immortal's demise,
the burninhunkaluv that never dies

snuffed out. We didn't hear it on BBC News
but in 60 wailing watts of ***G.I.Blues***

through an opened window, two, three times, then four,
then a knock-knock-knockin at our back door

half an hour later, *"He's dead, Mima, DEAD!"*
and my mother cradling a hairnetted head;

and a houseworked-to-death other-world of women clapped
momentarily. Then the record stopped.

Seeing her cry made all of us cry, too,
so we bansheed for Rock 'n Roll's Waterloo.

Going upstairs, not knowing why I felt so thrawn,
I browsed the collection, thanked God for The Stones,

Muddy Waters, BB, Sonny Boy and Chuck Berry
- and the black men, forgotten still in delta poverty.

(I cursed you then, Elvis, cursed that rockin and rollin,
never knowing the ***blues*** of the blues you'd stolen.)

And On High, sneering down from Housewife's Heaven,
you're perfect - the secret sin, unshriven.

Stuart A. Paterson

Prestwick Airport

Here the world's great walked on our common ground,
though we had history before they came:
Wallace once stood upon a nearby mound
to watch the well-stocked barns of Ayr aflame.
When I was young, they called it Orangefield:
Ball and McCudden used to fly from here,
flat western farmland of the fogless bield [1]
long before radar made dark heaven clear.
Now to new fields the flying galleons sail,
tracing their glide-paths over city walls.
Where once the Sleeping Warrior marked the trail, [2]
the ghosts of queueing phantoms haunt the halls.

But here, among the phantoms and the blues,
Elvis touched Scotland once in G.I. shoes.

1 - bield: shelter, protection (Scots)
2 -Sleeping Warrior: the outline of Arran

William Neill

Elvis: The poem

Bounty hunter
from my far West
he gyrated
into TV town
and holed up at
Heartbreak Hotel,
the guitar-slinger
with a lip sneer
for whom madams
and molls grew moist
at a wriggle of
his little finger.

Eds and Ellas frowned,
others thumped Bibles
as he cleaned up in
Nashville's saloons
where no one rolled
a hip faster.
On every wall
his name and mug-shot
- the most wanted man,
before fast food,
ice-cream soddened him.
Tears on Boot Hill.

Best remember
the lanky kid
casual against a
gas pump in Memphis
while, behind him, the
pick-up truck idles.
On its front seat
an old strum box
warming in the day
and climbing sky-high
the sun's gold disc
not yet in his sights.

Wes Magee

Big Sister's Former Boyfriends

You know, that loose gang of gaggly lads
That hung around our back gate, or sat
Thin-bummed on the front wall ledged
Between railing stumps cut down
For the war effort, those lads in jitterbug
Shoes, drainpipe slacks, crew cuts -
All bravado and cup-handed smokers:

"Presley" Smith, the Elvis of the town
With his blue suede shoes and moody looks,
Cedric with his sudden carrot-red,
Ray and his nine-inch dick (or so
My sister whispered to me one night, her eyes
Widening, and fingers spanning into light)
Or Jim who passed me scrappy notes
For her with SWALK scrawled raungily
In black Quink ink, and Geoff who leant
On doorjambs asking Mum in practised
Nonchalance if Mags was coming out.

Seeing them twenty years on,
"Presley" hush-puppying round dance halls
In smooching croons or trying since his
Baby left him to grind some square tango round,
Cedric with his ratting-cap, Ray sporting
Lump-pushing cords, Jim ground down with
His postman's round and Geoff the joiner
With nicotined hands, helps me understand
Why she picked the lad with Pat Boone
Teeth and fresh American looks, who never
Smoked and had all things in proportion.

True, he's spawned a gut and has perhaps
More hair (combed forward), not to mention
Bungalow, two kids, two cars, and though
He suffers from vertigo (too much worrying
Over this bank balance?) he still has all his teeth.

(Our Mags keeps hers all night
Grinning acidly in a glass.)

Seeing them, seeing her, seeing him
I cringe at how I might have become to them
That soft prick of a milk-tooth kid
Now lead saxophone in Lonely Street's
Heartbreak Hotel.

Roger Elkin

Hound Dog

Corn starch boy,
rich in the devil's music,
hungry for silk shirts, Cadillacs.

Curtis had a slicker D.A.,
Mitch a surlier lip.
Brando's eyes were meaner.

But your thirst was so fierce
that you howled it
stronger than anybody.

Hanging out in Beale Street
with B.B.King.
Mumbling all James Dean's lines -

Before the Colonel screwed you up,
the silly groans, the vibrato
soiled your clean hard tenor.

Not the first poor white
to die in his own puke

remembering Vernon and Gladys

offering Jesse Garon
a peanut butter sandwich.

Patricia Pogson

Naked Gun

when you dream
of Priscilla

we who love
tenderly

ask

are you
policeman

or paedophile?

Kerry Sowerby

Missing Elvis

First time round I missed out
on Elvis - too whirled off my feet
by my own circular skirt to notice;
how my new pony-tail flicked and hung.

So I ducked the shock of Rock
and Roll. I was turned on enough
just by wearing stilettos, how walking
was down to my hips, the way they swung.

I must have heard ***Heartbreak Hotel***
sobbed above the hubbub of pubs, words
pumped out through velvet. Visceral. I picked up
the beat, but missed the implications,

far too carried away by kissing
itself to go further; with applying my sugar-
pink-candyfloss lipstick ready to be licked off;
sheer exploration of mouths, teeth, tongues.

Decades later, living through
a different fifties, now kisses mean more
or less than themselves. And I'm glad
not to miss him, this second time round,

as my twenty-year-old daughter
and her boyfriend stick up his picture, sleep
together beneath his surprisingly familiar
lop-sided brooding; imitate his rhythms,

his fingering, his cowslick. While I
ransack Oxfam for signed photos to send them,
those records I wish I'd possessed; only now
feel his coarse beauty's oddly innocent appeal.

Frances Wilson

Hyperglycaemic Haiku

You were high alright
on noise and lights - and candy
flossing through your veins

Hilary Mellon

The King of Rock and Mime

Joanna is in the garden harvesting psychic strawberries
Her fingers the black of piano keys
Dressed in a full-length skirt that tickles her ankles
And high heels that dig into the soil
Above the long, red-brown bodies of worms
Daffodil bulbs glow in the dark.

Absorbed, she does not hear the postman deliver a letter
To the old address at the Institute of Evolution
Dear Joanna, long lung-distant graduate academy of breath
On the mat that says *welcome* it lies there
A frustrated guest forever unopened
By the person to whom it does relate.

Joanna would haunt for clotted cream, tequila sunrise,
Pistachios from the supermarket, silver spoons and china,
Wimbledon on the wireless, Ladies' Day on the patio,
Someone to scratch her ruby-red lips
And sometimes call her Demelza.
Ever since he died she's had a crush on Elvis.
Before Elvis it was Beethoven,
Before Beethoven, a lorry driver from Kansas.
Now she listens to Elvis singing rhythm and blues
Down behind the herbaceous borders,
Her fingers improvise boogie-woogie
On an old upright on the patio in the rain.

The next-door neighbour's cat saunters sensuously
Onto the patio and brushes herself against nothing
Punk electric fur stands up like needles
A feline crackle despite the rainfall.

Joanna spends the dark hours when consciousness
Lapses into dreamtime
Browsing through memory notebooks of unpublished poems
Hand-penned historical artefacts
Breast blessed, Memes children
Now writing nightly in invisible ink her new work
Is washed off the air by the eventual light of morning
On accidental tunnels made by birds the cat sent over.

At dawn she watches several species of troubadors
Fly off to discover such faraway fables
As Africa and America
Her one-day wish is to travel with them
Queue at the angel's desk, collect a pilot's passport
Be adopted by a family of cuckoos.
Already she's learnt to walk through walls
Without being stuck or bringing down plaster.

As the seasons fan their consequences on sky and soil
And the wind shares cloud and tide duties with the moon
And the rain and the rain repeats itself.

Joanna stretches her piano fingers over black and white keys
Playing lonesome lost love blues when
the King of Rock and Mime
Meets the Queen of Baroque and Roll.
Elvis is in the cabbage patch, humming a medley
Of Dixie Chicken and The Ace of Luck.
Sometimes when sweeping the path he imagines
The broomstick to be an acoustic guitar
Or in the greenhouse's glass booth
Thrashes out innuendoes and chords
When the poet plays piano on the patio in the rain
And the rain and the rain repeats itself.

Kenny Knight

from The Great Gig in the Sky:

The Backing Band Tune Up

... Jimi tunes
                                    the **e** string
to an **a**,
                          turns up the volume
on Vox
                        and Strat,
                                                     plays feed-
back
                  like an angel.

Another Jim,
                                        ex-Doors,
lets the bass
                                         bleed
                                                           slowly.

Moon is crazy
(as usual)
and Brian
riffs rhythm,
is stoned
and relaxed
as

is Janis,
on the wing,
practising
harmonies,
badly ...

And the dead
are waiting
waiting
for the King.

Steve Davies

Elvis Presley Discusses the Nature of Reality/Love in the Age of Intelligent Machines

(With dialogue from ***Girls Girls Girls*** *- 1962)*

why is it you feel so much more
al - ive in a storm? she says

while we
indulge in antique rituals
the touching of alien skin
the ceremonies of probing
dried folds and apertures
of flesh, making love
with the T.V. on

I don't know, I guess maybe it's
because everything seems more
intense, more real, says Elvis

while we
indulge in ancient ceremonies
of waiting, of penetration
of silence, of shifting
of engulfings and
barren devourings

this is real, she says
yes, says Elvis

while we indulge in
withered games of breathing
that leave us just as empty
and withdrawals that leave
the same vacuum, the same
unease that remains
as intangible

you sound doubtful, she says
you're not too real yourself,
says Elvis

words that are just as
unformed and unspoken

not yet, she says

Andrew Darlington

Dialogue by Edward Anhalt/Allan Weiss reproduced by kind permission of Paramount Pictures.

Painkillers

The King of rock 'n' roll
grown pudgy, almost matronly,
Fatty in gold lamé,
mad King encircled
by a court of guards, suffering
delusions about assassination,
obsessed by guns, fearing
rivalry and revolt

popping his skin
with massive hits of painkiller

dying at forty-two.

What was the pain?
Pain had been the colours
of the bad boy with the sneer.

The story of pain, of separation,
was the divine comedy
he had translated
from black into white.

For white children too
the act of naming the pain
unsheathed
a keen joy at the heart of it.

Here they are still!
the disobedient
who keep a culture alive
by subverting it, turning
for example a subway
into a garden of graffiti.

But the puffy King
lived on, his painkillers
neutralizing, neutralizing,
until he became
ludicrous in performance.

The enthroned cannot revolt.
What was the pain
he needed to kill
if not the ultimate pain

of feeling no pain?

Thom Gunn

Dick Boulton
paints and digs the garden in Upper Norwood, just round the corner from where Pissaro used to live. Over the past 13 years, he's had 27 one-man exhibitions in London galleries and in the provinces; his work has also been shown at the Royal Academy. For the cover of this book, he drew Elvis from memory, not from photographs.

Phil Bowen
was born in 1949 in Liverpool, where he worked as a Drama teacher for several years before becoming a publican in and around the West Country. Widely published in magazines and anthologies, he is the author of **The Professor's Boots** *(Westwords, 1994)* and editor of **Jewels and Binoculars** *(Stride/Westwords, 1993)* - a Bob Dylan-related anthology that triggered this collection. But that's another story.

Tilla Brading
is a freelance writer, poet and teacher. Her poetry has appeared in a variety of magazines and she has published two books for children: **Pirates** *(Macdonald)* and **Pirates & Buccaneers** *(Wayland)*. She is reviews editor and trouble-shooter for Odyssey magazine.

Tony Charles
didn't start listening to Elvis until his elder sister lost interest, but often still sings ***A Fool Such As I*** in the toilet. Widely published, various awards, residencies. Editor of **Headlock**. Fourth collection, **Carvings** *(Odyssey)* emerged recently.

Steve Chubb
was born in Islington in '64, now lives opposite Stan Laurel's birthplace in Cumbria and does Goegraphy and guiter (only one of these with any competence). He dreams of writing a long poem and of playing 3rd guitar for XTC or the Blue Aeroplanes. Dream on.

John Cornelius
was born in Liverpool in 1949, but now lives in London. Vocalist, songwriter & guitarist; artist & author. Interests/influences include "beat" writers, R&B, Bob Dylan, Henry Miller, art, poetry, gardening. Claims to be "Criminally underpublished", is nonetheless represented in **Liverpool 8** *(John Murray.* He's also appeared in mags, newspapers and anthologies and has shared in two volumes of poetry: **Endless Rain** (with Frank Duffy) and **A Bit of England** (with Dave Iveson).

David Crystal
was born in Prudhoe, Northumberland in 1963; now lives in London. He's a poet and the editor of **Dog**. His work has appeared in various magazines and a booklet, **The Bettle House**, will appear shortly under the *Clocktower* imprint.

Tim Cumming
was born in 1963, lives and works in London. He has wide representation in magazines and two collections published - **The Miniature Estate** *(Smith/Doorstop)* and **Apocalypso** *(Scratch)*. Read last year in the **New Voices** season at the South Bank Centre

Andrew Darlington
is an SF and music journalist and stand-up poet who'd like to have been Elvis's love-child. The first single he ever bought was ***Mess of Blues*** and his first LP was Vol 1 of the ***Elvis' Golden Records*** set. And he still has both. He once shook hands with Robert Plant, who once shook hands with Elvis.

Steve Davies
is 44. Ex- Merchant seaman, helicopter test engineer and whatever, he's now a social worker in Somerset. Poetry in several magazines and broadcast on Radio 4; his first collection, **Flowers from the Slag Hills** *(Littlewood)* will be followed by a second next year. He collects whatever takes his fancy at the moment and plays very loud music with a local band. Most of his heroes are dead, including Sid Vicious and D.H.Lawrence. Live ones include Dennis Skinner.

Roger Elkin
is a Staffordshire lad born and bred, and teaches at Leek College. A prolific poet and an indefatigable competition entrant, he has been the recipient of a large number of prizes and awards; his work is widely published, including a collection, **Pricking Out** *(Aquila, 1988).* The co-editor of **Prospice** for some years, he is now editor of **Envoi**.

Damian Furniss
read comic books as a kid. So did Elvis, whose favourite was Captain Marvel Junior: he adopted his quiff and sideburns. Damian has had many hairstyles, that included. Elvis had a twin, Jesse, who died at birth. Damian has three sisters, one brother. Elvis's mother was called Gladys Love. Damian's is Sheila Rosina. Damian is 26. So was Elvis once. Is Damian Furniss Elvis Presley?

John Gibbens
was born in Cheshire while Elvis was in the Army, and got to Germany just after he left. Elvis was playing hotels in the desert while John was at school in the Lakes and their paths didn't cross again until about 1980, when John found out what a great musician Elvis was - amongst other things, he reckons, the funniest of singers.

Ann Gray
came to Cornwall via London, Cambridge and Italy and to Elvis, late and reluctantly, via Cliff. She now cares for the Frail Elderly, which is just a co-incidence. She's been frequently published in magazines, and has a collection due out later this year. Also a dancer, she collaborated with Attic Dance on the dance poem **Sometimes**, which toured the Midlands and South West in 1992.

Thom Gunn
emerged in the late 'fifties as one of the most important poets of his generation; books such as **My Sad Captains** secured his reputation for combining tight writing with current idioms and preoccupations. His most recent collection, **The Man With Night Sweats**, won the Forward prize and restored him to the forefront of contemporary writing. His **Elvis Presley** was probably the first major poem about Elvis ever published; appropriately, it opens this volume.

Geoff Hattersley
was born in 1956 and lives in Elsecar, South Yorkshire. His poems have been widely published over the past ten years. Most recently he appeared in the *Bloodaxe* anthologies **The New Poetry** (1993) and **Poetry with an Edge** (2nd edn, 1993), and published a volume of new and selected poems with *Bloodaxe,* **Don't Worry** (1994). With his wife, Jeanette, he edits and publishes **The Wide Skirt.**

Gwen Jones
spent most of her first 25 years in Devon, but drifted away in search of life; having found rather too much of it, she accidentally returned to Essex, where she'd been born in 1946. Since 1991, her poetry has been published in nearly twenty magazines and her first collection, **At the Barrier** (Rockingham Press) came out in 1993.

Kenny Knight
lives and writes in Plymouth, where he was one of the founder-editors of the beautifully-named mag, **Terrible Work**.

Genista Lewes
began her career as an actress, now teaches, and performs her poetry in and beyond the West Country. Her work has been in magazines, in the national press and on radio. She first encountered Elvis at a sleazy party where his sensuality and style transfigured the surroundings. But, No, she didn't keep a pair of blue suede shoes on her shelf and wouldn't ever dream of screaming.

Jim Lindop
Born in Slough in 1942 within earshot of Betjeman's sad invective, Jim Lindop became a rocker in 1956 on hearing the opening riff to ***Don't Be Cruel*** at massive distortion on the dodgems at the fairground that came to Granville Playing Fields once a year. He played in a rock 'n roll band in Bristol for a few years. Now, described by Peter Mortimer as "an anecdotal guitarist-cum-businessman", he writes occasional verse and lives in Essex with his wife, Sue.

Ian McDonough
was born in Brora, Sutherland in '55, lives in Edinburgh & is a Citizens' Rights worker. Published in a number of Scottish poetry mags, he is a member of Edinburgh Shore Poets and is represented in **The Golden Goose Hours** *(Taranis, 1994)*. He likes Elvis very much, but likes Captain Beefheart even better.

Ian McMillan
is a widely-published and anthologised poet, who has edited for **The Wide Skirt** and **Iron** as well as leading memorable workshops. He is probably best known for his performances with Martyn Wiley, the other half of **Yakkety-Yak.** "Absolute madness", said the Guardian - and they can't be wrong, can they?

Wes Magee
Born Greenock, Scotland, 1939: a former bank clerk, National serviceman, teacher; now a full-time author who's published four collections of poetry for adults (latest, **Flesh, or Money**, *1991*) and over forty books - fiction, poetry, plays, anthologies, etc. - for children, most recently **The Scibblers of Scumbagg School** *(Orchard, 1993).*

Hilary Mellon
Born in 1949 in Norwich, where she still lives; 21 years in Science labs until redundancy struck, a late mother and slow burner who's almost finished an OU degree (begun in 1982). Now a part-time creative writing tutor; widely published in mags and anthologies; first full collection, **Disturbing the Night** *(Envoi, 1989)* shortly to be followed by a second from *Headlock.* And, as a schoolgirl, she went around with Hank B Marvin's name written on her thigh in biro......

Martin Mooney
took a bit of tracking down. He's Belfast-born (1964 vintage) and is at present a member of faculty at Poet's House, Co. Antrim. Publications include pamphlets and, most recently, **Grub** (Blackstaff, 1993), which was shortlisted for both the Ruth Hadden Memorial and the Forward prizes. Watch out for **Rasputin's Children**, currently in preparation.

William Neill,
one of the major Scottish poets of his generation, was born in 1922 at Prestwick, Ayrshire, which happens to be the only place where Elvis ever stood on British soil. He writes in Gaelic, Scots and English and has published eleven collections of poetry, most recently **Tales Frae the Odyssey** *(Saltire Society, 1992)*. A former winner of the Sloane Verse Prize, the Grierson Verse Prize and the SAC Book Award; his **Collected Poems** are to be published this year by *Canongate.*

Stuart A. Paterson
was born 28 years ago in *Kernow* but is Scottish as *brochan*. Prefers the folk music of The Battlefield Band and Wolfstone to what he calls the "stolen blues" of Elvis, but is not beyond redemption. Gets very excited when speaking of Kate Bush. Has a rapidly growing reputation as a poet, won a Gregory award in 1992 and a Scottish Arts Council bursary in 1993. Lives in Ayrshire, where he edits **Spectrum** and is kind to cats but not posing poetasters.

Patricia Pogson
began publishing 15 years ago and has featured widely in mags and anthologies. Her most recent collections are **Rattling the Handle** *(Littlewood)* and **A Crackle from the Larder** *(Redbeck)*. Watch out for **The Tides in the Basin**, coming soon from *Flambard.*

Jeremy Reed
is a major voice amongst contemporary poets, with many collections to his credit. He is also a novelist, whose latest book, **Diamond Nebula** *(Peter Owen, 1994)*, is described by J.G.Ballard as "an elegant and poetic newsreel". His new collection of poems, **Pop Stars** (from Entharmon), also comes well recommended. He lives and writes in London.

Joe Shortt
was born in a small Irish town you won't have heard of. He studied Art in Dublin and printmaking in Geneva; then he tried his luck in Paris. After spending all his money on paint, he ended up in Barrow, where he now teaches. He has a burgeoning reputation as a painter, lithographer and illustrator, and exhibits regularly.

Penelope Shuttle
was born in Staines in 1947, now lives in Cornwall with husband Peter Redgrove and daughter Zoe. Widely anthologised, including **Penguin Book of Contemporary British Poetry** and **Sixty Women Poets**. Her most recent collection was **Taxing the Rain** *(OUP, 1992)*; she has also published five novels. Her pioneering collaborative text (with Peter Redgrove) on menstruation, **The Wise Wound**, is re-issued from *Harper Collins* in June 1994.

Mal Smith
never met Elvis, but knows a woman who says she did. He currently leads a double life as student at Central School of Speech and Drama and siinger/songwriter in the world's greatest undiscovered rock band. He likes long-haired, green-eyed women and sparkly-white satin jumpsuits, and is inspired by Steve Phelps.

Steve Sneyd
was a teenager himself when Elvis' career began; although his first record purchase was ***Rock Around the Clock***, many Presley releases soon joined it. Like millions of that generation, he felt Elvis' death both as a personal loss and an intimation of mortality. Internationally-published poet and short-story writer: his collected poems, **In Coils of Earthen Hold**, is published by *University of Salzburg* (1993). Founder member, Science Fiction Poetry Association.

Kerry Sowerby
was born in Co Durham, lived in Cumbria and then Royal Leamington Spa. Unsurprisingly, he moved to Leeds because he thought there must be more to life; there wasn't; so he founded the magazine **Ramraid Extraordinaire.**

Ray Stebbing
is a semi-retired FE teacher, having previously worked in industrial research and in technical/scientific publishing - for that nice Mr Maxwell. He's now furiously writing poems in an attempt to make up time wasted on these frivolous pursuits. Regularly published, he has a slim volume, **Travelling Man**, out from *Approach poets.*

Geoff Stevens,
longtime editor of **Purple Patch**, grew up Wild in the (Black) Country of south Staffordshire before it became a Heartbreak Motel at the hub of the motorways. The first rock he encountered was slag from the iron furnaces, the second was Presley's from Sun Records.

Gordon Wardman
is a poet and novelist. Check out **High Country Hank** *(Odyssey, 1993)* and **The Newfoundland Cantos** *(Headlock Press, 1994)*. He's also had failed careers as probation officer, revolutionary, family counsellor, etc. An ageing redneck, he approves of Elvis' drug abuse, OTT ballads and understated dress sense. Like Elvis, he lives in Harlow, Essex, country capital of the UK.

Anthony Watts
has had many poems published in magazines and anthologies, has won several awards including an Arvon Foundation Prize (1982) and gives readings at various venues & festivals. His first collection, **Strange Gold** *(KQBX, 1991)*, is shortly to be followed by a second. He also runs the Fire River Poets group in Taunton.

Frances Wilson
lives, writes, teaches and paints in Ware, Hertfordshire. She's had poems published in many magazines and stories broadcast on radio; she's also a keen competition entrant whose successes include second in the National Poetry Competition in 1990. Her first collection, **Close to Home**, was published last year by *Rockingham Press.*

Jim C. Wilson
On 16th July 1958, Jim C. Wilson saw Elvis in ***Loving You*** at the Grand Cinema, Edinburgh. He hasn't been quite the same since. However, in 1981, Wilson decide he'd never be a pop star, so became a writer. His second poetry collection, **Cellos In Hell** *(Chapman)* appeared in 1993. Wilson is now 45, lives in Edinburgh, and still strums stubbornly at his guitar.

Rodney Wood:
"I'm married with two grown-up children and work in London. I never heard Elvis records much when very young but pre teens I used to go to the pictures once a week. Elvis was my hero, who boxed and dived from great heights - did he really need a stuntman? At nights I used to dream that he was my brother; until, that is, my mother started to like him."

Derek Woodcock
was born in Jarrow in 1949 and currently works as an English teacher on South Tyneside. He is frequently published in magazines around the country.

King's Crown

......but in our times, the crown lies hidden, waiting for the King himself to come again and claim his kingdom.......